BACK TO THE BIBLE

BACK TO THE BIBLE

J A Gallimore

Book Guild Publishing
Sussex, England

First published in Great Britain in 2006 by
The Book Guild Ltd,
25 High Street,
Lewes, East Sussex
BN7 2LU

Typesetting in Times by
IML Typographers, Birkenhead, Merseyside

Printed in Great Britain by
CPI Bath

A catalogue record for this book is available from
The British Library.

ISBN 1 84624 040 9

Contents

v

The Bible is a book of two parts: the Old Testament, which is the revelation of God throughout history from the beginning of time to the birth of his Son, Jesus Christ and the New Testament, which is the record of the birth, life, teaching and death of Jesus Christ. Much of the Old Testament would at first reading appear irrelevant and would not appear to have a spiritual meaning, but its value as part of the whole book is that it supplies the atmosphere and background for the development of religion. It advances a history in which is integrated religion and ethics written by religious authors who have no peers in modern times. It includes much of lasting value which is not repeated in the New Testament. However, without the Old Testament the New Testament would be bereft of some of its authority. The Old Testament includes the ancestry of Jesus from the first man, Adam, and predicts what is to happen to the Son of God.
The New Testament is written by men chosen by Jesus to be his followers.

J. A. Gallimore

1

The Truth of the Bible

Throughout the last 1,000 years so-called experts in theological studies have spent their energy trying to prove that the Bible is untrue or at least is mythological based. Many stories in the Old Testament cannot be verified but archaeologists are finding more and more evidence that the details recorded are correct. Dr E.K. Pearce in his book *Archaeology* lists many examples where critics have censured the accounts in the Bible but which have now been found to be correct. Following are a few which he lists.

The critics said that Moses could not have written the first five books in the Bible because writing had not been developed during his lifetime. Nowadays many stone tablets inscribed with cruciform scripts have been discovered which were written before the time of Abraham, thus proving that writing was available well before the time of Moses.

In Joshua 10 a battle is reported in which Joshua needed extra time to defeat his enemies before darkness fell. So he appealed to God for the sun to remain shining for sufficient time to rout his enemies. The sun shone from midday for a whole 24 hours. The critics said it was impossible for an extra day to be added to the calendar. However, Heroditus, the great historian of ancient times, writes that the Priest of Egypt showed him in their records the existence of an unusual long day. Professor Totten has stated that a whole day of 24 hours has been inserted into worlds history. E.W. Maunder, Fellow of the Royal Astronomical Society, has traced the exact spot where Joshua stood and determined the date and time of day where the phenomenon took place. Even computer programs have found that an extra day has been added to the calendar.

The book of Jonah tells the story of how he was swallowed by a whale. 'Impossible,' said the cynics. They argue that a gill in the front of its mouth prevents any other than tiny fish entering its throat. What the unbelievers do not appreciate is that there are 14 types of whale, some of which can swallow large-sized objects. Apparently there are three cases where seamen have been swallowed alive and survived, either by regurgitation or by the whale being cut up.

In Genesis 19 there is the story of God raining fire and brimstone on the cities of Sodom and Gomerra, completely destroying them. A television writer and many other critics said that the story was untrue. However, archaeologists and other scientists have discovered the location of the ruined cities and found sufficient evidence to prove the Bible story is true. Salt deposits are also incorporated, thus verifying that Lot's wife could have been changed into a pillar of salt.

The crossing of the Nile by the children of Israel and the fall of the Tower of Babel have all been verified.

In fact, no story in the Old Testament has yet been proved to be a fake, or mythical. Hence it follows that all records are likely to be true.

Considering the New Testament, it is probably true to say that more research has been carried out to verify its truth than any other historical record. Even today, historians are attempting to find possible errors in the writing.

The Dead Sea Scrolls verified the wording of the Bible and so sceptics suggest that they were put in place deliberately to show that Christ was invented. However research of the Scrolls has shown their veracity.

The Gospel by St Luke has been criticised severely. One argument being that in 3:1 it says that in the 15th year of Tiberius Caesar, Lysanias was tetrarch of Abilene and this was a mistake. The 15th year of Tiberius was 27 AD and Lysanias was put to death years before then and he was not a tetrarch (ruler) but a King. Fortunately for the truth of the Bible, a gentleman by the name of Nymphaeus dedicated a pagan temple in Abilia and an inscription telling his story was found there. The Inscription included a title 'The Lords Imperial' which was one used for the Emperor Tiberius and Livia (his Mother) and it was carved during the reigns of the two rulers (i.e. between 14 AD and 29 AD). Nympaeus is quoted as a 'freeman of Lysanias the tetrarch'. Clearly there was a second Lysanias and he was tetrarch to Abilene, exactly as Luke said, and he lived during the period suggested by Luke.

Some critics of the Bible suggest that it was not necessary for Joseph and Mary to travel to Bethlehem for the birth of Jesus. However, it has been established that the Romans had a periodic enrolment of Egypt and Syra every 14 years so that the statement by St Luke that everyone had to go to his own city which was thought unnecessary has now been confirmed. A decree has been discovered in 104 AD with the above order and it was worded as if it was a usual custom and hence the necessary return of Joseph and Mary to Bethlehem has been confirmed.

Regarding the reference to feeding the 5,000 by Jesus, St Mark says Jesus went into the desert privately. But apparently he was followed by a large crowd. This was a contradiction, say the critics. However, St John in his Gospel says it was the time of the Passover and many people would be coming and going at Capernaum and crowds would follow Jesus even though it was intended as a private exercise.

Critics say that the fourth Gospel and the Book of Revelation could not both have been written by St John since the Gospel is in good Greek whereas Revelation is abrupt

3

and with numerous faults in grammar. They said that a Galilean fisherman like John was insufficiently educated to have written the fourth Gospel. The explanation is that the Gospel was written with the help of a Greek disciple whereas Revelation was written at Patmos where he was not likely to have had friends and hence little help.

J.B. Phillips, the translator of the New Testament, said that the more he worked on the Bible the more convinced he became that the New Testament was true. He said that the letters by St Paul could not have been written if there had been no Jesus Christ – no crucifixion and no resurrection.

Billy Graham, the great Christian Crusader, had no doubts about the truth of the Bible. He said, 'Its critics who claimed it to be filled with forgery, fiction and unfilled promises are finding that the difficulties lie with themselves and not the Bible and more careful scholarship has shown that the apparent contradictions were caused by incorrect trans-lations rather than divine inconsistencies. It was man and not the Bible that needed correcting. It is the blueprint of a Master Architect. The true Christian denies no part nor attempts to add anything to the word of God.'

'The following recording of a radio programme in 1996 describes the Bible in detail. The author of the programme is unknown.

This book contains the mind of God, the state of man, the way of salvation, the doom of sinners and the happiness of believers.

Its doctrines are holy, its precepts are binding, its histories are true, and its decisions are immutable.

Read it to be wise, believe it to be safe, and practise it to be holy.

It contains light to direct you, food to support you and comfort to cheer you. It is a traveller's map, the pilgrim's word and Christian's charter. Here paradise is restored, heaven opened, and the gates of Hell disclosed. Christ is its grand subject, our good is its design and the glory of God is its end.

It should fill the memory, rule the heart and guide the feet, read it slowly frequently, and prayerfully.

It is a mine of wealth, a paradise of glory and a river of pleasure.

It is given you in life, will be opened in the judgement and will be remembered forever.

It involves the highest responsibilities, rewards the greatest labours and will condemn all who trifle with its contents.

The Bible then, is inerrant (Psalm 119:160), indestructible (Matthew 24:35) incorruptible (1 Peter 1:23) indispensable (Deuteronomy 8:3), infallible (Matthew 5:18), and inexhaustible (Psalm 92:5).

What other book can provide stories that children can read and enjoy and at the same time provide material for research for the intellectuals of the country?

What other book can provide such a comforting passage as the 23rd Psalm?

The Lord is my shepherd; I shall not want
He maketh me to lie down in green pastures: he leadeth me beside still waters.
He restoreth my soul: he leadeth me in the paths of righteousness for his name's sake.
Yea, though I walk through the valley of the shadow of death, I will fear no evil: for thou art with me; thy rod and staff they comfort me.
Thou preparest a table before me in the presence of mine enemies:
Thou anointest my head with oil; my cup runneth over.
Surely goodness and mercy shall follow me all the days of my life: and I will dwell in the house of the Lord for ever.'

2

Prophecies

All the predictions in the Old Testament were written before the time of Christ. This fact is indisputed since they have been preserved by the Jews themselves, who are opposed to Christianity, and hence would not alter the records to show any favour towards Christ.

Consider the predictions concerning the life and death of Christ:

Isaiah 7:14
Behold, a virgin shall conceive and bear a son and shall call his name Immanuel.

Exactly as it happened.

Isaiah 52–13 to 53–12
He shall be exalted and extolled and be very high

It is generally admitted that the teaching and conduct of Christ were of the highest order

As many were astonished at thee, his visage was so marred more than any man and his form more than the sons of man

His death on the Cross was public and the cruel method of his death must have disfigured his face and body.

Kings shall shut their mouths at him for that which had not been told them shall they see and that which had not heard shall they understand.	Kings are nowadays in reverence of his conduct and teaching
Who hath believed our report and to whom is the arm of the lord revealed?	The prophet reveals an unbelievable presence in the person of Jesus.
For he grew up before him as a tender plant and a root out of dry ground; he hath no form or comeliness and when we see him there is no beauty we would desire him	Jesus lived in Nazareth, which was regarded as dry ground, and his appearance was such that at his trial when Pilate presented him to the people they refused him.
He was despised and rejected of man, a man of sorrows and acquainted with grief and we hid as it were our faces from him and we esteemed him not	This explains what is to happen at his trial and crucifixion
Surely he hath borne our grief and carried our sorrows yet we did esteem him stricken, smitten of God and afflicted	Knowing he would be crucified at an early age, his life was one of grief and sorrow his crucifixion would appear to him to be accursed of God
He was wounded for our transgressions he was bruised for our iniquities; the chastisement of our	This refers to his scourging and illtreatment, nails driven into his hands and feet, and the wounding with a spear.

peace was upon him; and with
his stripes we are healed

All we have gone astray; we   Thus did Jesus take
have turned everyone to his   upon himself to atone the
own way and the Lord hath   sins of all
laid on him the iniquity of
us all.

He was oppressed, yet he   He refused to plead
humbled himself and   at either of his trials
opened not his mouth as a   and bore ill treatment
lamb that is led to the   patiently
slaughter and as a sheep that
before her shearers is dumb;
yet he opened not his mouth.

They made his grave with   He died between two
the wicked and with the rich   robbers and yet he was
in his death   buried in a rich man's grave.

Yet it pleased the Lord to   After his suffering
bruise him; he hath put him   and death, he rose
to grief: when thou shalt   again, prolonging his
make his soul an offering   days in the pleasure
for sin, he shall see his seed,   of God
he shall prolong his days
and the pleasure of the
Lord shall prosper in his
hand

Therefore will I divide him   This is clearly a
a portion with the great and   reference to his triumph
he shall divide the spoil with   in the Christian Church
the strong.

| Because he poured out his soul unto death | His was a voluntary lingering death and the mental realisation that he had to bear the sins of others was surely extremely painful. |
| And was numbered with transgressors yet he bear the sin of many and made intercession for the transgressors | His last words on the cross 'Father forgive them' was forgiveness for all of us. |

Its also interesting to note that Psalm 22 foretells the happenings at the crucifixion.

The words 'My God, my God, why has thou forsaken me?' were repeated by Christ on the cross.

'All they that see me laugh me to scorn: they shout out the lip, they shake their head saying, "He trusted on the Lord that he would deliver him."' This was a true indication of what happened.

'They part my garments among them and cast lots upon my vesture.' As carried out by the Roman soldiers.

'They pierced my hands and my feet.'

Of course the cynics would say that Jesus, having read the Old Testament, would attempt to make the predictions come true.

However, he could not have arranged to be born in Bethlehem.

He could not have arranged to be crucified since the usual method of execution with Jews was by stoning.

He could not have arranged to die between two robbers (i.e. he made his grave with the wicked).

He could not have arranged to be put in a rich man's grave (with the rich man in his death).

He could not have arranged for his garments to be gambled for (as arranged by the Roman soldiers).

Prophecies relating to Jews

Consider the following extracts from the Old Testament; Ezekiel 22:15. I will scatter thee among the heathen and disperse thee in countries.

Hosea 9:17 My God will cast them away because they did not hearken unto him and they shall be wanderers among nations.

Amos 9:9. For lo, I will command and I will sift the house of Israel among all nations like a corn is sifted in a sieve.

Deuteronomy 28:7. The Lord shall cause them to be smitten before thine enemies, thou shalt go out one way against them and flee seven ways before them; and shalt be removed into all the Kingdoms of the earth.

Considering these predictions, what actually happened to the Jewish Nation?

When Jesus Christ was alive there was a thriving Jewish nation in the land of Israel. Previously it had been part of the Roman Empire and the Jews did not like being governed by foreigners and they fought at least three wars of independence. However, each time they were defeated and in 70 AD the Romans decided to stop the revolts once and for all. They completely destroyed Jerusalem, ploughed up its site and sent the inhabitants of Judaea (main part of the land of Israel) into exile.

For century after century the Jews survived as a nation without a country. Wherever they went they were hated and treated as an inferior race and often forced to live in ghettoes.

Consider the treatment they received in England:

Jews first appeared in England in the reign of William the Conqueror but they were never welcome and in 1190 massacres spread from city to city, wiping out Jewish men, women and children.

In 1290 Edward 1 expelled all Jews from Britain.

In 1492 some Jews who had been expelled from Spain

came to live secretly in England. They were always in fear of their lives in case they should be found out. In 1656 Jews were eventually readmitted to England by Oliver Cromwell. However, they were always treated as second-class citizens.

In 1858 Jews were finally allowed to sit in Britain's Parliament.

For 17 centuries the exiled Jews were persecuted, massacred or made to flee from one country to another.

Following are further predictions relating to a return to their own land.

Jeremiah 30:11. For I am with thee though I make a full end of all nations whither I have scattered thee yet will I not make a full end of thee.

Hosea 3:5. Afterwards shall the children of Israel return.

Ezekiel 11:17. I will even gather you from the people and assemble you out of the countries where you have been scattered and I will give you the land of Israel.

Ezekiel 36:24. For I will take you from among the heathen and gather you out of all countries, and will bring you into your own land.

All these prophecies have been verified. Since 1,800 years after being exiled from their own country they began to trickle back and eventually over 2,000,000 set up an independent state of Israel. It is interesting to note that as predicted in Leviticus 26:23–35 the original land belonging to the Israeli people was made waste when they left. Even the enemies of the Jews did not take advantage of the abandoned land until the first half of the 20th Century.

It is interesting to note that in Genesis 27:29 and Genesis 12:3 God said of Israel, 'Cursed be every one that curseth thee and blessed be he that blesseth thee' and applying this statement to recent events.

During the 1930s Hitler and the Nazis had made plans to conquer the world. By 1940 everything had gone to plan and the German war machine had conquered most of Western

Europe. Yet within five years Nazis Germany had ceased to exist and Hitler had committed suicide. Why? Many people suggest that Hitler had overruled his experts and hence made the wrong decisions. Some Christians would say that God said 'cursed be those who cursed the Jews'. By planning to wipe out the Jewish race the Germans were challenging God. It is also interesting to note that after the war the new German government gave hundreds of millions of pounds to the Jewish Nation, even though their own country was in tatters and much of their youth was dead. They did not lose by their generosity since by the 1970s they were one of the richest countries in Europe (blessed be to he that blesses them).

There are many more prophecies in the Old Testament which would appear to have been verified.

In Exodus 6:6 God promises to deliver the children of Israel from the Egyptians. It takes many torments for the Egyptian people before the children of Israel are allowed to march to the river Nile and face what appears to be an impossible barrier. A strong wind blew continually until a path was created across the river so that they could cross and thus fulfil God's prophecy. At one time critics of the Bible said such a happening was impossible, but in 1936 the flow of the Nile was restricted again.

Jericho was an exceedingly evil city, worshipping false gods, killing babies to appease evil spirits and so on. God wished to destroy the city, but it was a strongly-walled place. Joshua, who had been chosen to lead the assault had no means to break the walls down. However, God told him to march his men round the city on each day for six days, but on the seventh day to march round seven times and then make a loud noise and the walls would collapse. It happened exactly as God expected and Joshua and his men took possession quite easily. A curse was laid on the city and no building has been completed on the site since.

Isaiah 40:22 describes the world as being round. The word

used is 'circle' (The word 'round', being translated to 'circle' in the Hebrew language). In Job 26:7 the 'earth hangeth in nothing'. How did these prophets explain the shape and suspension in space of the earth nearly 3,000 years ago?

Consider the prediction relating to Job's writing in Job 38:31. 'Canst thou bind the sweet influence of Pleiades or loose the bands of Orion'? How did Job know the names of these constellations when the telescope and observatory were not invented until the 17th century?

It is interesting to note the reference 'sweet influence' to Pleiades. The *Oxford Reference Dictionary* refers to the Pleiades cluster of stars as a 'beautiful association'

Orion is often associated with 'Orion's Belt' which is suggested by the bands of Orion.

Finally consider the prophecies of St Peter explaining what he wrote about the attitude of people nowadays.

2 Peter 3:3 and 4
'Knowing this first, that there shall come in the last days scoffers, walking after their own lusts and saying, Where is the promise of his coming? For since the fathers fell asleep, all things continue as they were from the beginning of the creation.

(Here Peter is prophesying that people will mock at the idea of Jesus returning. In his day most people would have accepted that Jesus would return but Peter knew that people 1,000 years later would scoff at the idea.)

People nowadays would say that Jesus could not return because it would be against the natural way of events since all things will continue in their present form.

2 Peter 3:5 and 6
For this they willingly are ignorant of, that by the word of God the heavens were old, and the earth standing out of the

14

water and in the water; Whereby the world that then was being overflowed with water perished.

(In Peter's day the reality of the Flood was never questioned whereas nowadays, 1,400 years later it is considered by many scientists to be a myth, which is exactly what he predicts.)

2 Peter 3:10
But the day of the Lord will come as a thief in the night; in which the heavens shall pass away with a great noise, and the elements shall melt with fervent heat, the earth also and the works that are there shall be burned up.

(In Peter's day the most dangerous sources of heat would be the burning of combustible materials. How did he know that almost two thousand years after his death there would be incendiary bombs, napalm, and atom bombs?)

It will be clear that all the prophecies listed must have been inspired by God.

3

Miracles

It would seem the prerogative of some teachers of religious knowledge in schools to explain that Jesus was a good magician and the miracles he performed were simply happenings that any good magician could reproduce.

Consider the following explanations by the sceptics and the reasons why they are wrong.

(1) Converting Water into Wine

Apparently pouring water into a container used previously for holding wine enables the water to absorb remnants of the wine and become wine again. I wonder if the winemakers throughout the world understand this effect. According to the critics providing the correct material is used for the wine bottles it is possible to double the output of wine and according to the Bible the second wine is better than the first. Since the second wine is better, its remnants will be an improvement and hence a third filling of bottles will make an even finer wine. What nonsense!

In any case, Jesus did not use the containers used for wine but pots which had been placed near to the entrance of the house to contain water used for washing hands and feet of the visitors.

(2) Feeding the Five Thousand

This miracle was one of the few recorded in all four gospels so it is likely to be a true record. However, the critics suggest that all the people took their own sandwiches. But the people had spontaneously followed Jesus and his Disciples. According to the Bible record, the people had no food of their own and apostles suggested they should be allowed to disperse into the adjacent villages to get victuals. They had been away from home for three days. But Jesus said no and asked how much food was available. Only five loaves and two small fishes were available and these he used to feed the five thousand. As an example of economy Jesus asked for the remains to be collected, resulting in 12 full baskets, much more than would be available if everyone had taken their own food.

(3) Miraculous draught of fishes

The cynical explanation of this miracle was that Jesus saw a large shoal of fish from the shore which the fishermen apparently had missed, but Jesus told the fishermen to 'launch out into the deep'. This indicates that the fish were caught in the middle of the lake which Jesus could not have possibly seen from the shore.

(4) Walking on Water

The critics explain the miracle of Jesus walking on water by saying he was walking on a ridge of sand or on the surface of a breakwater. But since he walked to a boat which was in the middle of the sea such an explanation is nonsense. There would not be a ridge of sand, or a breakwater in the middle of the sea. To prove the point, Peter jumped from the boat and sank almost immediately. An experienced sailor such as Peter would have known the existence of any aid to treading on the water.

(5) Lazarus raised from the dead

According to the cynics the simple explanation for this miracle is that Lazarus appeared from the dead by hiding in his grave until Jesus came. This explanation is most improbable because the two sisters of Lazarus were genuinely grieving and the people must have known he was dead because he was wrapped in grave clothes when he emerged from the grave. Jesus had deliberately waited four days, when surely knowing his friend was entombed he would have arrived much earlier.

It must be appreciated that all the miracles were carried out by Jesus with many witnesses present. They were never disputed, even though enemies as well as friends were present. He cured people of many illnesses. He made the blind to see, the dumb able to speak and the deaf able to hear and any deception would have easily been noted. He was able to cure people at a distance and without personal contact as he did for the Centurion's servant and the woman of Canaan's daughter. No magician could have done these things and certainly no magician could have quietened a storm as Jesus did.

Some people ask why there are no miracles nowadays. But there are. Doctors and nurses will give examples where patients with pronounced terminal illnesses still recovered.

Consider the following example:

The Reverend Roy Harthern from Stoke-on-Trent was so ill his kidneys had stopped working, cancer ravaged his body and his blood pressure was ultra low, enough to kill him. He persisted in studying the verses in the Bible concerned with divine healing for hours on end. Suddenly his health returned. The doctor told him a miracle had taken place, his kidneys were brand new and functioning normally and the cancer had disappeared.

During the Second World War two happenings could be considered as due to God's assistance. During the evacuation of our troops from Dunkirk the sea was calmer than had been known for that time of the year, thus helping our soldiers to escape. At a critical phase in the Battle of Britain the wind was so strong against the invading German planes it slowed them down to allow the defending airmen time to regroup.

4

Problems with God and Heaven

Christians are often asked how do we know there is a God and where is Heaven.

The problem with Heaven is that there does not appear to be any place for it to exist. One theory suggests that earth and heaven are moving along parallel lines which never meet and have no physical connection. However, its situation is unimportant if we can somehow accept that God exists.

Again, it is difficult to appreciate that there is a being who can oversee what every person on the earth is thinking or doing at a particular time.

When we consider what we mortals can accomplish with computers it becomes less of a problem to appreciate what our Heavenly Father can accomplish. After all, he has designed our brains, enabling us to carry out amazing mental operations which we would have thought impossible 50 years ago. So there doesn't seem any problem with understanding what God can do since he created us.

Clearly there is no way we can prove the existence of God except by noting the existence and behaviour of his son, Jesus Christ. If Jesus did exist and he was a good man we should take note of what he said.

In other words we ask three questions.

(1)   Did Jesus Christ exist?

(2)   Was he a good man?

(3)   If he was a good man should we not believe what he said since a good man would not tell lies?

(1) Did Jesus Christ exist?

There is more evidence of his existence than anyone else of his time. Many men of distinction have set out to prove he was a myth and always they have proved he did actually live. The evidence of his life is shown overwhelmingly in the gospels. It is most unlikely that he could have been invented. The Jews were expecting a Messiah and Jesus did not live up to their hopes. The Gentiles had no use for him either, theirs was a cruel selfish world and Jesus did not fit into their mode of life.

(2) Was Christ a good man?

A study of the scriptures will show that Jesus led a blameless life. In his perfect moral teaching there was not the slightest evidence of sin. He never accepted he had need for self-righteousness even though he blames others for submitting to such an attitude. He taught people to love each other. When suffering, because of men, he never lost his temper even when he was mocked and cruelly treated during his crucifixion. To demonstrate his humility he even washed the feet of his disciples. He never rejected the cry of the sufferer or refused to answer the questions of the faithful.

Dean Farrar in his book the *Life of Christ* indicates the effect Jesus had after his lifetime.

'The effects then of the work of Christ are even to the unbeliever indisputable and historical. It expelled cruelty; it curbed passion, it branded suicide; it punished and repressed an execrable infanticide; it drove the shameless impurities of heathendom into a congenial darkness. There was hardly a class whose wrongs it did not remedy. It rescued the gladiator; it freed the slave; it protected the captive; it nursed the sick; it sheltered the orphan; it elevated woman; it shrouded as with a halo of sacred innocence the tender years of a child. In every region of life its ameliorating influence was felt. It changed pity from vice to virtue. It elevated poverty from a curse into a beatitude. It ennobled labour from a vulgarity into a dignity and a duty. It sanctified marriage from little more than a burdensome convention into little less than a blessed sacrament. It revealed for the first the angelic beauty of a purity of which man had despaired and of a meekness at which they had utterly scoffed. It created the very conception of charity and broadened the limits of its obligation from the narrow circle of a neighbourhood to the widest horizons of the race. And while it thus evolved the idea of humanity as a common brotherhood even when its tidings were not believed. All over the world wherever its tidings were believed, it cleansed the life and elevated the soul of each individual man. And in all lands where it has moulded the characters of its true believers it has created hearts so pure and lives so peaceful, and homes so sweet that it might seem as those angels who had heralded its advent had also whispered to every depressed and despairing sufferer among the sons of man

'Surely a man who caused all this graciousness in the world must have been a good man'

(3) Why should we not believe what he said? A few of his sayings are now listed;

'For when two or three are gathered together in my name there am I in the midst.'

'Heaven and earth shall pass away but my words shall not pass away.'

'And lo, I am with you always, even to the end of the world.'

'Are not five sparrows sold for two farthings and not one is forgotten before God.'

'For God so loved the world he gave his only begotten son, that whosoever believeth in him should not perish but have everlasting life.'

'In my father's house are many mansions; if it were not so I would have told you. I go to prepare a place for you.'

The only way we can deny the existence of God is by saying that Jesus was a hoax. Can anyone who has read the Bible say this?

5

Wickedness in the Bible

Critics of the Bible will point out that many stories from the Old Testament can be considered cruel and barbaric. God appears to have ordered wicked deeds, sanctioned wicked customs and even approved of wicked men.

God is recorded as having organised the destruction of Sodom and Gomorrah, Jericho, the Canaanites, as well as other minor groups of people. The reason he found it necessary was due to the wickedness of the people involved. In addition to all kinds of immorality, they carried out human sacrifices, including the murder of children. They worshipped strange gods and God had no alternative but to teach these people a lesson and stop their wicked behaviour. The critics would say it was wrong to kill everybody since there would be children and well-behaved people involved. But the innocent may have been spared. For example, Lot and his wife were allowed to escape from Sodom and Gomorrah, and Rahab, her father, mother and all her kindred escaped the catastrophe at Jericho so that other people might have escaped punishment without their absence being recorded.

The only survivors of the flood were Noah and his family and this would seem to be unfair to the rest of mankind. However, according to Genesis 6:12 there is recorded 'And God looked upon the earth and behold it was corrupt of all flesh ... Only Noah and his family were good living people and hence the rest had to suffer. Scientists are still arguing as to whether the flood was a local affair or a world-wide occurrence. If it was only local one not many people would have been involved.

God Sanctioned bad behaviour?

The critics of the Bible point out that God encouraged his favoured men to have more than one wife. Solomon and David were typical examples. Solomon had many wives in his harem and David had a few. However, it is not true to say that God encouraged these affairs. He expected monogamy but relaxed the rules when he realised it was difficult to adhere to ideal principles. Certainly David was punished by the death of his beloved son.

There are many examples in the Old Testament where a man had only one wife: Isaac and Rebekah and Boaz and Ruth were typical examples. The Old Testament set out the idea of marriage: one man and one woman joined together as one.

It can be noted that in the Old Testament God's judgement on wicked people was carried out instantly in the form of natural disasters such as earthquakes, floods, plagues, etc, whereas in the New Testament the punishment comes later.

There are examples of supposed wickedness in the New Testament. Probably the most baffling case is that of the betrayal of Jesus by Judas Iscariot. Judas was one of the apostles of Jesus. He must have had free will, since we are all free to do what we want and yet he must have been a wicked man to sell his friend for 30 pieces of silver. Critics will say that God arranged for him to do what he did but in reality all that God did was to arrange the timing of the betrayal. In other words, he did not develop the action but directed it for his own purposes.

The destruction of the barren Fig Tree by Jesus allows the critics to say what a stupid, petulant man Jesus was and how he could exhibit anger, impatience and vengeance at times.

26

Apparently figs can be taken from the tree for most of the year. Early in the year there are the late (previous year's) fruit and later on the new growth, both of which are eatable. In the case under consideration there was no fruit at all so that it had been barren and hence useless for two years. But Jesus who had refused the tempter's offer to 'turn stones into bread', could not be accused to have 'flown into a rage' at one barren tree. In fact, what he did was done with a very good reason. He did it to teach the Jews a very vital lesson. To the Jews the fig tree was a symbol of the Jewish nation (see Hosea 9:10 and Joel 1:7) and in his parable Luke 13:6–9 he indicates that a fig tree which does not bear fruit should be cut down. Hence his destruction of the fig tree was demonstrating the uselessness of the Jewish Nation and his failure to convert them. In fact, they were preparing to crucify him.

There are many incidents where scribes and pharisees acted wickedly. One example concerns the woman caught in adultery: Jesus was in the temple with a large number of people when the scribes and pharisees brought in a woman caught in adultery, thus subjecting her to the stares and curiosity of all those present and making, with total disregard for her feelings, a pawn in their hatred for Jesus. In other words, they were simply using her to put Jesus in a difficult position. They asked Jesus what they should do with her. If he aquitted her he could be considered as guilty of heresy because the law said she should be stoned to death. If he suggested she be allowed to go, he would be convicted of sedition. Jesus simply resolved the situation by saying 'Let him that is without sin among you cast the first stone.'

The worst case of wickedness, of course, was the crucifixion of Jesus Christ.

6

The Ten Commandments

The Ten Commandments, Exodus:20, make up what is called the Christian Duty, in other words, not only what we ought to do to be a Christian but realise what we owe to God.

Unfortunately, they are becoming of less importance by the existing population and even some clergy refrain from reading them out during communion services. However, they are just as relevant today as when they were spoken, to Moses on Mount Sinai on the occasion of the escape of the Israelites from Egypt.

1st Commandment: (One God) 'I am the Lord thy God which have brought thee out of the land of Egypt; out of the house of bondage. Thou shalt have no other Gods but me.' God was reminding the Israelites what he had done for them. He had saved them from slavery, pain and death by bringing them out of Egypt and he was instructing them as to what they could do for him. The Israelites were moving from the Egyptians, who worshipped many Gods, to Canaanites who also believed in polytheism so that it was necessary to remind them there was only one God. This commandment is just as important today since we may not imagine other beings for us to worship but we can, without realising it, develop targets which attract the whole of our interest. For example, a miser makes savings his god, a drunkard allows alcohol to become his one interest in life and so on. There is no harm in saving or drinking, providing the exercise does not become obsessive.

2nd Commandment: (True Worship) 'Thou shalt have no other gods but me. Thou shalt not make unto thee any graven image, or any likeness of anything that is in heaven above or that is in the earth beneath or that is in the water under the earth. Thou shalt not bow down to them, nor serve them: for I the Lord thy God am a jealous God visiting the iniquity of the fathers upon the children unto the third and fourth generation of them that hate me: and showing mercy unto thousands of them that love me and keep my commandments.'

We are told that man was made in the image of God but this commandment says we should pray to God, not to his image. Neither should we make idols and pay service to them. Thankfully, the use of idols and praying to false Gods is gradually dying out in the developed countries so that we should concern ourselves with the correct approach to God and, if a focal point is necessary, use that of Jesus Christ.

3rd Commandment: (Reverence) 'Thou shalt not take the name of thy Lord in vain: for the Lord will not hold him guiltless that taketh his name in vain.' God's name must be hallowed, never spoken lightly, used in swearing or thoughtless jest … If in a court of Justice a witness swears to speak the truth and calls God to witness, this is a correct use of God's name If, however, he asks God to witness and then swears falsely that is taking God's name in vain and God will not hold him guiltless. Using God's name when carelessly attesting is also forbidden; some people use God's name to make their words sound truthful and this is also wrong. Cursing and swearing with God's name involved is very sinful. Using the name of Jesus in the same way is also against the wishes of God.

4th Commandment: (Holy Times and Seasons) 'Remember the Sabbath day to keep it holy. Six days shalt thou labour, and do all thy work, but the seventh day is the Sabbath of the Lord thy God.'

Nowadays, sport and business have begun to operate on Sundays to the extent that there is little difference between the various days of the week. Some people have to work on Sundays: hospital staff, farmers, travel operators etc. but others choose to do so. It is arguable that mowing the lawn, cleaning the car, gardening etc. is labour since people say they enjoy this kind of weekend work. However, no matter how involved, most people can take it easy and manage to attend a church service during the day. There is a considerable difference between a holiday and a holy day and Sunday should be considered as the latter, a day that belongs to God. Whether we have to work, choose to entertain ourselves, or simply remain idle we should make an extra special effort to worship God on his day.

5th Commandment: (Obedience) 'Honour thy Father and thy Mother; that thy days may be long upon the land which the Lord thy God giveth thee.' This is the only commandment with a promise. The question arises as to what 'honour' means. Maybe it can be expressed in three words 'love', 'obey' and 'succour'. It should be natural to love our parents but do we love them enough? Of course some parents are inhuman, in which case it may not be possible to honour them since love is a two-way exercise. But we must try to love our parents as ourselves whenever possible. Until we are as wise as they it is only appropriate for us to take their advice. If they are good parents they will certainly be concerned to provide the best for our welfare. The time will come as our parents grow old they will need help and it is our duty to provide that help in their latter years.

6th Commandment: (Innocence) 'Thou shalt do no murder.' This commandment could be expanded to 'do not hurt anybody by word or deed.' It is sinful and unlawful to take the life of someone else. But it is also wrong to make someone else feel miserable by physically hurting them or criticising or making them feel inferior, particularly so if they become tired of life. We should never feel envious of other people since envy can sometimes lead to murder. Cain killed Abel, David killed Uriah and Ahab killed Naboth all because of envy and there are plenty of incidences nowadays when envy results in murder. There are cases when killing can be justified. A just war can lead to a good man killing another good man. If countries or factions are fighting each other one side may be considered as blameless and hence soldiers on this side may have to follow orders. However, they must know they are fighting a just war.

7th Commandment: (Purity) 'Thou shalt not commit adultery.' God says our body is a sacred thing and the temple of his spirit. If we defile our body he will not hold us guiltless. If a man takes another man's wife he is not only sinning himself, but causing the woman to sin as well. No man can avoid seeing women other than his own wife, and no doubt be attracted to them, but he must say no to any temptation to corrupt his body. It is said that 'the body is a good servant but a bad master' and it follows that people should be the master of their body and retain it in cleanliness and godliness.

8th Commandment: (Honesty) 'Thou shalt not steal.' When we reach our hand to take what does not belong to us we are breaking this commandment. We should all know that we are stealing when we are taking from someone that which belongs to them and which they have worked hard to get or bought with savings accumulated over a long time. Some people think taking minor items should not be considered as stealing. Taking an apple from someone's orchard, taking a pen from the office and taking a piece of chalk from school are all considered as stealing and could lead to greater sins. We must do our work honestly, pay honestly for what we get and give honestly. It could be considered as stealing if we keep anything back which should be passed on. If we find a wallet it should be given up since it does not belong to us. To give good weight, and good measure are essential actions of a Christian.

9th Commandment: (Truth) 'Thou shalt not bear false witness against thy neighbour.'

This commandment is concerned with the 'word' . A man may use his words to soothe, anger, explain, confuse, please, to encourage, to convince and to lead. It follows that one should be careful always to speak the truth and give the best advice possible. The expression 'think before you speak' is very good advice since half the problems in the world are due to people speaking hastily. There are many occasions when saying the wrong thing is sinful. If a person is applying for a job and has been given a false testimonial or reference then this is dishonest. We should never repeat unreliable stories about someone. We should never lie, never tell tales and never resort to slander. The only safe way to speak is to tell the truth, the whole truth and nothing but the truth.

10th Commandment: (Be content with what you have) 'Thou shalt not covet thy neighbour's house, thou shalt not covet thy neighbour's wife, nor his manservant nor his maidservant, nor his ox, nor his ass, nor anything that is thy neighbour's.'

It is difficult to go through life without wanting something we cannot have, but the sin is to let the desire rule our lives. In other words, if it is not possible for us to have a specific thing we should not let the desire stay in our mind. Just as a bad action is a sin, a desire can be considered as ungodliness. It is not wrong to want wages for our work, but it is wrong to want payment for something we are not prepared to complete. It is not wrong to want something from a shop for which we can afford to pay but the question is do we really need it or could the money be put to better use. St Paul in Philippians 4:11 said, 'I have learned in whatsoever state I am in therewith to be content.' Considering all the trials and hardships he had undergone, this was a remarkable statement and is an example for all of us.

Summating the Ten Commandments
The one word that the commandments demand is 'love'.
If we love God we would not consider any other God.
If we love God we would worship him without fail.
If we love God we will not take his name in vain.
If we love God we should honour the day he asks us to respect.
If we love our parents we would be pleased to obey and succour them.
If we love our neighbours we would never think of murdering them.
If we love our neighbours we would never want to corrupt them.
If we love our neighbours we would never think of stealing from them.
If we love our neighbours we would never tell untruths about them.
If we love our neighbours we would never want something they would want to keep.

7

Bible Puzzles

The Bible is not a puzzle book but cynics who study the Bible are always ready to point out incidents which are difficult to understand.

Following are a few of the most common puzzles.

Adam was the first man on earth yet his son Cain was able to find a wife. Where did this woman come from?

Reading the bible in Genesis 1:27 we are told that God created man, so that human beings were around before Adam. It follows that Adam and Eve were simply the first couple on earth to be specifically named. Some authorities claim that Cain married his sister but this is unlikely. Many Christians consider death as the result of the disobedience of Adam and Eve (usually considered as 'the Fall') because in Genesis 3:3 God said, 'Ye shall not eat of the fruit of the tree in midst (of the garden of Eden) neither shall you touch it lest ye die.' Although Adam ate from the tree he lived to be 930 years old. One explanation is that the interpretation of the word 'die' meant originally as a distancing from God and not physical death.

The flood causes many problems for some. How could two of all the creatures in the world be contained in an ark about 150 yards long 25 yards wide and 15 yards high and be fed and cleaned for nearly a year? How could they be collected in the first place? How would the penguins from the

Antarctic manage to travel the length of the world? It was certainly a large ark, but even so, to consider two of every known animal to be involved stretches the imagination. There are two possible explanations: firstly the flood might have involved only a local area and hence the creatures easily dealt with. If the world-wide flood is involved it could be that only one representative of each class of animal was involved and not each variety. For example, chimpanzee, gorilla and orang-utan all developed from a common ape ancestor. Maybe all the various cats could have had one ancestor and so on. As far as food was concerned, the animals could have been in hibernation and hence none required. Scientists would say that all these developments happened well before the flood but they have been known to be wrong before.

One unusual project is explained in Genesis 11:1–9.

It was known as the Tower of Babel and archaeologists have determined where it happened, thus proving it was an actual event. Apparently at the time there was only one language throughout the whole earth and the people of Shinar wanted to keep it that way. So they decided to build a city with a tower that would reach up to Heaven. But God decided they were trying to usurp his authority and so he confounded their one language, resulting in many languages, and scattered the people abroad to stop their insurgence against him, so the tower was never complete.

In the New Testament the puzzle is: why did God organise such a complicated book. Why are four apostles allowed to give their own versions of the same happenings when one gospel might have shown more authority?

Consider two of the reasons where the apostles differ:

The first one regards the notice which appeared at the resurrection:

(Matt 27:37) Matthew writes : This is Jesus the King of the Jews

36

(Mark) 15–26 Mark writes: The King of the Jews
(Luke) 23–38 Luke writes: This is the King of the Jews
(John) 19–19 John writes: Jesus of Nazareth the King of the Jews

These writings would suggest that each apostle is simply writing his own version of what he thought should have appeared. But as John explained, the notice was written in three languages, Hebrew, Greek and Latin, and the wording could have been slightly different in each language. When we consider that Matthew was writing for the Jews, Mark for the Romans, Luke was a Greek writing for the Greeks and John was concerned with inner meanings of the scriptures rather than events, there is no surprise at the different versions of the notice.

A second example where the critics point out the conflict occurring at the birth of Jesus. Matthew says the family went to Egypt and stayed there until the death of Herod. (Matthew 2:13–15. Luke says they went to Jerusalem for a short visit and then to Nazareth which is in the opposite direction from Egypt. Luke 2:22 & 39) However, by reading the episodes carefully it is noticed that Matthew and Luke are describing two different episodes in the story. Luke says the shepherds visit him in the stable where he was born and refers to him as a 'Babe'. On the other hand Matthew tells how the wise men had to make a long journey and by the time they arrived Jesus was a 'young child'. Hence the reports which are apparently contradictory are at different periods.

There are many instances in the Bible when reports of the same occurrence vary considerably. However, there are not many apparent contradictions which cannot be explained in different languages. The fact that there are four gospels with sometimes different reports tends to prove the genuineness of the writings. Had they all been very similar one could have assumed collaboration.

Now consider the Bible Code.

For many years it has been suggested that there is a code using letters in the Bible to predict important happenings.

The code uses the first five books of the Hebrew bible and the predictions are found by laying out the entire text in one continuous strand. By searching the letters for hidden words or phrases which appear when an equal number of letters are omitted, messages can be read. It was Professor Eliyahu Rips who discovered the code. He is recognised by mathematicians around the world as a genius, a leading authority in group theory and a person who deals only with significant mathematical results.

On 1st September 1994 a message was passed to the prime minister of Israel, Yitzhak Rabin, to tell him that his name was encoded in the Bible with the words 'assassins that will assassinate' across his name. He was told that the assassinations of Anwar Sadat, and both John and Robert Kennedy, were also encoded in the Bible. He was warned that he was in real danger, and that he should take necessary precautions. On 4th November 1995 he was shot in the back and killed. He failed to take the precautions which had been suggested by Rips' work. This episode was just one prediction from the Bible code which proved its reliability.

The code demonstrated that the death of Princess Diana was encoded in one chapter of Genesis. The words 'Diana', 'Paris' they 'killed me' all appeared in the same place together with 'The Egyptian' and 'Engagement'. These words must have been encoded in the Bible 3,000 years before the accident happened. In addition to the prediction Diana's death, the start of the Gulf War was discovered before it actually started, every detail of the 9/11 attack on New York with the words 'Twin Towers', 'Airplane', 'Attack' and 'Twice' appeared in the code. Many people have tried to show that any book could provide such predictions but only by a random selection of letters and not spaced with an equal number. Any book will only enable happenings to be shown after they have happened, not before, as for the Bible code. The American code-breaker Harold Gans was a total sceptic when he started to study Pips' work but after a thorough investigation found that it did work. He even checked by finding the names of Jewish prophets with details of their births and where they were born. The chief of Mossad, the Israeli intelligence agency, and Yassar Arafat both accept the findings of the Bible code.

Surely the Bible must have been influenced by God. What other writer could organise stories and give clues to what is to happen in 3,000 years' time.

8

Prayer

When I was a boy it appeared to me that some people found praying rather difficult but to others it appeared very easy. It was rather puzzling until I realised there are many ways to pray and prayer is a personal process depending on our attitude to God.

A sister nun said on television that she prayed seven hours each day without using one word. In fact, she only used words when she was praying with someone else.

Kathleen Doreen Rogers (S.E.N) was on duty in the front line during the last war. She had three miraculous escapes from direct bombs hit and one from a land mine. She had a complete nervous breakdown. She began repeating the 23rd Psalm, 'The lord is my shepherd,' and she recovered.

Sometimes it is difficult to know what to pray for. During the last war Archbishop William Temple refused to pray for victory but the Archbishop of York Dr Garbett told his congregation to do so.

Some people find it difficult to pray. There is an old proverb which says, 'If you don't know how to pray you should go to sea in a small boat.' In other words, if we are in dire peril it is easy to ask for deliverance. However, in less extreme circumstances it may be difficult to find the right words. We should never ask for material things.

Robert Louis Stevenson's prayer was 'Give us courage,

gaiety and a quiet mind.' Courage is not necessarily the man who is never afraid, but the man who conquers fear. A non-Christian is miserable and without hope but a Christian is bearer of good news. To have a quiet mind we should always do the ethical thing so that we have nothing to fear, and able to look on fellow beings with nothing to be ashamed with.

Most prayers seem to remain unanswered and some find their appeals are not answered in the way they expected.

For example, if 100 soldiers are going into battle we could pray that they all return safely. Maybe a quarter of them would be killed but if we had not prayed, three quarters of them might have been killed.

A lady doctor appearing on television developed a cancerous leg as a child. She prayed fervently for it to get better. However, as it remained diseased she had to have it amputated. Apparently as an adult she agreed that her prayers had been answered but not in the way she expected. When she became a doctor she found having lost a leg meant that she could sympathise more readily with her patients.

There are at least 100 prayers mentioned in the Bible commencing with Abraham's prayer for Sodom (Genesis 18:22–23) to John's prayer for Gaius (3 John 2). In the Old Testament they are usually involved with the power of God asking for help but not necessarily for the petitioner's benefit. Following are just a few to illustrate the points.

In 1 Samuel: 7 Samuel prays for the Israelites.
In 1 Kings: 3 and 2 Chronicles: 1 Solomon prays for wisdom to judge God's people successfully.
In Job 10, Job asks the reason for his suffering.
In Nehemiah 1 he prays for the children of Israel.

One prayer which was answered to the petitioner's benefit occurs in 1 Samuel where Hannah, who had been childless asked God for a son. However, she had promised to give him over to God when he was grown up.

The first prayer in the New Testament is the Lord's Prayer in St Matthew 6:9–13 and St Luke 11:2–4. This prayer is discussed later.

In the Garden of Gethsemane Jesus asked God if it was possible for his crucifixion to be repealed, but he did add 'not as my will but as thou will' (Matthew 26:39).

He prays for his followers and all who will follow him (John 17)

St Paul prayed for the Christians at Rome, Israel, Corinthians, Ephesians, Phillippians and Thessalonians but not for himself.

Jesus taught his followers to pray using the Lord's Prayer as an example. Since that time it has been used as a heritage of every Christian liturgy. It is the best and purest of all prayers. It teaches us how to approach our Father in Heaven in forgiveness and selfishness. Only one petition refers to an earthly item: asking for food. Even this is sometimes translated as asking for spiritual guidance and support. One should follow the example of the Lord's prayer and try not to ask for material things. In fact, we should not pray for what we haven't got but pray that what we have is put to the best possible use.

Jesus instructed us how to pray: He said do not boast that you are praying, do not pray standing where you can be seen, pray in secret, do not simply repeat appeals continually.

Christians should not take heed of the experts who say 'that prayers are scientifically impossible, morally unacceptable, and of no avail'.

Prayers are said to be scientifically impossible because it would appear that God is interfering with nature. Suppose a man learns of a plane crash and, knowing his son was on board, prays for his safety. For his son to have been saved because of prayer God must have known the man was going to pray before the accident happened. In other words, it would have been God's foreknowledge that led him to answer the prayer. In every case God foreknows the result because of the man's conduct on which it depends. Which means that the answer to prayer may be regarded as divine coincidences, and not necessarily interference with nature, and not against scientific principles.

Prayer is said to be morally wrong since it is at variance with the power of God by suggesting he is partly under the control of man, downgrading his wisdom by suggesting he has to be informed of what we want and cannot be trusted to act for our best interests unless we interfere. But God takes an interest in our welfare and there is no reason why he should not be influenced by prayer. But God cannot be persuaded to change his will. Just as a human father cares for his child and refuses to give him all he asks for, God shows his goodness by providing most people with necessary blessings such as eyesight, good health etc. but depriving us of those things which are unnecessary. By refusing to give us some things which we may consider as requirements, God may be helping to fashion our character.

One moral difficulty arises when a person prays for the success of another. A person could pray for a friend to win a particular athletic race and if God organised him to succeed it could be said to be unfair to the rest of the competitors. But suppose if instead of praying for his friend to win the race he pays for him to have special training by an expert. Surely this is as hard on the others in the race who have no special help and yet the assistance could not be considered as unfair. It would seem that no matter how the runner is helped, the fairest way is by praying, since God would always act justly to all people. The prayer should only ask that the runner does his best and not necessarily win.

It is not true to say that prayers are of no avail. There are

44

many examples of people having their prayers answered as considered in the chapter on miracles.

Prayers have a greater effect when praying with other people. This is one of the reasons why it is necessary to attend at Church services.

An answer to a prayer can be considered as a miracle so that we cannot expect all our prayers to be answered. We can pray for someone who is ill to get better since this would be an ordinary natural course of events. But we can't expect miracles every time we pray.

Our prayers are of no avail unless we love God and are prepared to do his will and forgive all who have sinned against us.

We must also bear in mind that we never know when someone has prayed for us and hence show consideration to all people.

9

Sins and Forgiveness

We all sin and we all know when we are sinning. Only Jesus Christ led a life free from sin.

The workman charging an excess amount for his work may think it is good business but it is a sin and particularly so if the customer is distressed. The telling of lies and cheating to gain advantage are also sins, as are robbery, rape etc.

There are, of course, many degrees of sinning. Some sins are serious enough to be punished by the state, whereas others may be considered of little consequence.

The Radio padre who gave religious talks on radio during the last world war compared the degrees of sin with our handling of some practical object. For example, if we had a lawnmower it could be made useless by neglecting to oil the moving parts, leaving it outside in the weather to rust, or use a hammer to break it to pieces.

In other words, we could fail to do something which should be attended to, deliberately put something to one side which should be dealt with, or knowing what we are doing is wrong but deliberately carrying on. We, therefore, have the sin of not doing something which we know to be necessary, the sin of being stupid and ignorant and the sin of doing something which we know is seriously wrong.

We could kill a baby by not feeding it, by not keeping it warm and comfortable, or by poisoning it. So that if there is someone dear to you, you can sin by ignoring them, sin by saying you didn't know their condition, or by neglecting them completely.

These examples illustrate how the degree of sin can vary considerably.

We are able to sin because we have free will. If we couldn't do what we wanted to do we could not sin and there would be no wicked men. To decide whether an action is a sin or not we all have a conscience. This conscience tells us without any argument whether we are committing a sin or not. Just as the eye can distinguish between colours, our conscience can differentiate between good or bad behaviour. One of the most striking effects of a conscience is the feeling of remorse after wrongdoing. People may have different perspectives when deciding what is right and what is wrong but every person has his own conscience.

Some people do not appear to have a conscience and carry on misbehaving without regard for other people. They do have a conscience but go through life ignoring it. Some hardened criminals when caught will admit to all their crimes and accept they have a conscience by saying sorry for what they have done.

One reason why we should not sin is the effect it might have on other people. A man may experiment with drugs for a time and then become free from their influence. However, a second person who had joined in with him might carry on drug taking and persuade a third person to participate. Eventually there could be dozens of people taking drugs because of the person's actions and they could all have their characters destroyed.

The first person could say that drug misuse is not a sin but in destroying other people's lives it proved that it was. It follows that sin can have an infinite effect and should expect infinite punishment. Man himself could not pay the debt. He would be punished in one way in the case of the above example by seeing his friend dependent on drugs. But only Jesus could forgive such a calamity.

We should attempt to go through life without our conscience telling us that we are doing wrong.

Whenever we do sin we should ask for forgiveness.

Every sin deserves its punishment and the sinner needs to undergo some penalty, or to pay the debt, as it is called before he can justly be forgiven. To be forgiven the sinner must not only show he is genuinely sorry but show reparation for what he did. If a man robs a house he must not only say he is sorry but return all the articles he stole if he wants just forgiveness.

In one sense forgiveness could be a bad influence on the sinner. He could apparently sin throughout his lifetime since he has only to ask forgiveness when he is found out and since Jesus died for all our sins why bother? However, our sins will only be forgiven if we are genuinely sorry and ask for help to be so. If we were knocked down by a car and killed it might be too late to ask to be forgiven. If we lived on for a time it would be difficult to deal with all the sins we have committed. In Matthew 18 Peter once asked Jesus how many times he should forgive his brother for sinning against him. 'Seven times' he suggested. But Jesus said, 'Seventy seven times,' suggesting we always forgive people their sins providing they are really wanting our pardon. Jesus went on to quote the parable of the servant who having been forgiven by his king a debt of 1,000 talents, soon afterwards seized his fellow-servant by the throat and would not forgive him a debt of 100 pence, a sum 1,250,000 times as small as that which he himself had been forgiven. The first servant was placed into torment because of his lack of forgiveness, and Jesus said, 'So likewise shall my heavenly father do also unto you if ye from your hearts forgive not everyone his brother their trespasses.'

In other words, we cannot expect forgiveness for ourselves if we have not forgiven all those who have sinned against us and all the sins they have committed.

10

Sufferance

Many people cannot believe in a kind, caring God because of the suffering in the world.

Some people suffer continuous pain for long periods, children are ill-used and sometimes live a miserable and painful existence. Wars kill off many family members and some servicemen and women are injured for life. Earthquakes cause much suffering. Why does God allow such distress?

Pain is, of course, necessary. If we felt no pain we could put our hands in the fire and they would be burned to the bone. If we broke a leg there would be no urgency for attention and it would be deformed. Pain is usually a signal that something is wrong and indicates an illness which may be remedied with appropriate medical attention.

We must remember that the greater part of pain and misery in men is brought on by their own folly. In other words, God has given us free will and this is often misused. People bring trouble on themselves by smoking, drinking to excess, using drugs, consuming unsuitable food and being involved with exploits not appropriate for their bodies.

Pain and sorrow can also be due to the attentions of other people; murder, rape, torture, cruelty etc. and God cannot be blamed for what people do.

We still have the question why do good-living people have

to endure sufferance? One reason might be to form a person's character. If there was no suffering in the world, there would be no bravery, no patience, no compassion, no sympathy and no self-sacrifice for the good of others. In fact, without suffering there would be no character formation and no noble achievement.

There are examples of bravery recorded in the press daily, and also of people showing great patience and fortitude. Mrs Paul Carson, the wife of a missionary who was killed by the Congolese, said, 'Now they have no one to help them.' No recrimination, no bitterness, no comment about her two fatherless children, but all her sympathy was not for herself but for the Congolese who were involved in the savagery and cruelty prevalent at that time.

Many a soul has been brought to know God by the suffering and sacrifice of others. Felix Lesueur, the French atheist and hater of religion, turned to God when he found his wife had offered all her suffering for years for him. In her last will and testament she wrote, 'On the day I die I will have paid the price for your return to God.' Greater love than this no woman hath that she lay down her life for her husband. Anything is bearable providing a purpose is known. Just as the evil of man can influence, so good can influence for the better.

Many people have thanked God for pain and discomfort where it has meant a change in their lives and made them realise God is available. People do not always blame God for their suffering but have looked forward to meeting their maker.

One person whose suffering changed his life for the better was the Soviet novelist Alexander Solzhenitsyn. He was in prison for anti-Stalinist comments during his incarceration in the Soviet concentration camps of the Gulag he wrote, 'Bless you prison, bless you – for it was whilst lying on the rotting straw of my cell that I recognised the true purpose of life is not the progress of our materialism, but the progress of our souls.'

The one man in the Old Testament who really suffered was Job. In his time wealth was measured in the number of animals a person owned and he was a wealthy and important man. In fact, he was said to be the greatest man in all the east. However, in one day he lost all his animals, his oxen, asses, sheep and camels. Some were stolen and some burned by fire. The same day all his sons were killed and it would have appeared that God had organised his entire downfall.

However, he did not criticise God in any way. Later his whole body including his head, legs, and feet, were covered with boils making life extremely painful. His friends tried to make him censure God for his problems but he refused and still asked God to be forgiven for sins he had committed.

Jesus had no doubt what he thought about people who caused the suffering of children. He said, 'It were better for him that a millstone were hanged about his neck and cast into the sea than he should offend one of these little ones.'

We should remember that God allowed his son to meet a cruel death. We should also note that all his adult life he had to bear the knowledge that he would be crucified. Additionally, the leaders of his own church were his enemies and ever trying to destroy him by violence, and yet his final words before his crucifixion did not show recrimination of any kind, he simply said, 'Father forgive them for they know not what they do' (St Luke, 23:34).

In the book *Small Talks* by the Rev Ronald Selby Wright, S.C.F is a poem written by a soldier fighting in World War 2. It explains how the soldier in the fighting was helped to appreciate how Jesus suffered during his crucifixion and how he came to believe in him.

> Christ: I thought I knew all the answers,
> Until madmen started this war;

I never gave you a second thought
Nor ever talked to you before,
The age-old story of Bethlehem,
And the dream of Calvary
Were nothing more than fairy tales –
Yes, Lord mere fairy tales to me.

But to-night my helmet is heavy
And so is the pack on my back;
Barbed wire has left me two torn hands,
And my feet leave a bloody track.
My shoulders sag 'neath this heavy gun;
And my body is weary with pain;
And my whole tortured being cries out
For rest and release – but in vain.

For the first time in my life I know
Your head hurt from a thorny crown,
And your tired bleeding shoulders ached
When that heavy cross weighed you down.
Those nails cut into your hands and feet;
Every inch of your flesh was torn,
And your bruised body was weary;
My God – once you too were careworn.

But you didn't quit – you carried on
Until the grim battle was through,
And now I know you did it for me –
So I'll go on fighting – for you
I want you to know I'm sorry
It was my sins that put you to death;
And I'll keep on saying I'm sorry
Until I draw my last breath.

Christ: I never knew that war could be
The means of saving my soul;
How little I thought that I would find you –
In this muddy foxhole.

Death is inevitable for all of us. People in the prime of life are more afraid than older people, but no matter how frightening the thought of death appears if the time is known the more serene one becomes towards the end. Doctors and nurses who have seen hundreds die will all say that unless people have a guilty conscience they die peacefully and thankfully.

Even children who are aware of Jesus and Heaven look forward to death if they are seriously ill. Consider the following poem written by a 13-year-old boy who died of a brain tumour he had battled for four years. He died on the 14th December 1997.

He gave this poem to his mother. His name was Ben.

My First Christmas in Heaven.

I see the countless Christmas trees around the world
    below
With tiny lights, like Heaven's stars reflecting on the
    snow.

The sight is so spectacular, please wipe away the tear
For I am spending Christmas with Jesus this year.

I hear the many Christmas songs that people hold so
    dear
But the sounds of music can't compare with the
    Christmas choir up here.

I have no words to tell you the joy their voices bring
For it is beyond description to hear the angels sing.

I know how much you miss me, I see the pain inside
   your heart
But I am not so far away. We're really aren't apart.

So be happy for me, dear ones, you know I hold you
   dear
And be glad I'm spending Christmas with Jesus this
   year.

I sent you each a special gift from my Heavenly home
   above
I sent you each a memory of my undying love.

After all, love is a gift more precious than pure gold
It was always most important in the stories Jesus told.

Please love and keep each other, as my Father said to do
For I can't count the blessing or love he has for each of
   you .

So have a Merry Christmas and wipe away that tear
Remember I am spending Christmas with Jesus this
   year.

Anyone in suffering who believes in Jesus should remember
what he said in this context. In Matthew 11:28 he said,
'Come unto me all that travail and are heavy laden and I will
refresh you.'

11

Life after Death

Even some Christians have doubts about the possibility of
life after death. One problem arises as to the outcome of the
people in the various patterns of behaviour. It is usually
assumed that the good-living people go to Heaven and the
bad ones go down to Hell, but what happens to those who are
neither good nor bad? A lady I knew always insisted that
when we die we enter an intermediate state where some time
is spent before a decision is made. This idea does not seem to
be borne out by the Bible. In Luke 23:43 the thief being
crucified is told by Jesus. 'Today shalt thou be with me in
paradise.' In other word, the robber was transported into
Heaven because he accepted Jesus before he was killed. This
idea that a last minute conversion is acceptable is borne out
by the parable of the labourers in the vineyard (Matthew 20)
where those who had worked only a short time were given
the same reward as those who had toiled all day. This would
seem to be unfair since a person such as Mother Teresa
would get the same result for working for God all her
lifetime as a person who had misbehaved all his life except at
the end. Maybe there is a hierarchy in heaven which would
even things out, but it must also be remembered that Mother
Teresa enjoyed the love of God all her life and the man with
his misdeeds would no doubt have spent a miserable
existence.

A hierarchy in Heaven is suggested by the writing of the prophet Malachi. In Malachi 3:17 he writes, 'And they shall be mine saith the Lord of hosts, in that day when I make up my jewels.' When a jeweller is making a decorative item such as a necklace or a bangle he chooses his best jewel as a centrepiece and the less worthy ones in a surrounding pattern. Maybe Malachi was suggesting that God deals similarly with his chosen ones.

It is difficult to believe a person with a brain capable of understanding the difference between good and bad, appreciate music, being kind and considerate, acting bravely, probably sacrificing one's own life for some good purpose is suddenly cut off at death. Jesus knew there was life after death, he was always referring to his Father in Heaven, and proved an afterlife by appearing to many people after his resurrection. He hinted to his followers that they would follow him. In fact he said, In my Father's house are many mansions I go to prepare a place for you.'

Many people have been convinced of afterlife by being contacted by those who have been dead some time. Sometimes it is an actual appearance and sometimes it is a feeling of support from, someone they have loved.

In the book *Ring of Truth* by J.B. Phillips, the great New Testament translator, he talks of an incident whilst watching television. The late author C.S. Lewis appeared sitting in a chair near to him and spoke a few words relevant to the difficult times he was passing through. He appeared again when Phillips was in bed.

Many people have reported that they felt some late loved one was with them, particularly in times of stress.

Professor C.A. Coulsop F.R.S., Ph.D., M.A., D.Sc., Rouse Hall professor of Mathematics at Oxford, said he felt his mother's presence after she had died. 'Utterly real,' he said, 'is this life a broken pillar in a churchyard to show what might have been? 'Is it tears and sorrow and frustration?' Not

58

to those who know the love of Christ. In the words of the hymn by Richard Baxter:

> My knowledge of that life is small
> The eye of faith is dim
> But 'tis enough that Christ knows all
> And I shall be with him.

People do not contemplate their own death, although it is the one event certain to happen. One question we ask, 'Will we be able to recognise those we have loved on earth'. The apostles were able to recognise Jesus after his resurrection and maybe in our post-death physical appearance we shall easily recognise those we knew.

A grandfather who knew his grandson as a child at the time of his own death would be meeting his grandson as a grown man. But even on earth the situation would present no problem: a grandson could lose contact with his grandfather for a long period of time and later return as an adult to be reunited with his family.

Some people have been so close to death that doctors have considered them as being dead but somehow they have recovered. Their experiences have been such that they have enjoyed after life for a short time. On their return to life the happiness they have known means they will be happy to die when the time comes.

Doctors and nurses say that unless a person is mindful of some guilty actions he or she will be able to die peacefully.

12

Decline of the influence of the Church of England

Some events that would appear to have caused a decline in the influence of the Church of England:

1987 Lambeth Palace spokesman said, 'There is no place in the Church of England for homophobia.'
1991 Dr Lloyd Davies (Honorary Physician to the Queen) and D.C. Bourne (senior anaesthetist to the Salisbury Coronary) both suggest that Jesus did not die on the cross.
1994 David Jenkins, Bishop of Durham, gave the impression that he did not believe in the Virgin Birth.
1995 Church of England Board for Social Responsibility said, 'Living in sin is no longer sinful.'
1997 Richard Holloway, Bishop of Edinburgh, suggested modern behaviour, no matter how, against the teaching of the Bible, should be accepted.
1999 Dr George Carey, Archbishop of Canterbury (supported by the Church) cast doubt on the Resurrection.

(i) No Place in the Church for Homophobia

Any Christian reading Leviticus 20:13 and Romans 1:27 will be left in no doubt that the Bible considers homosexual relations to be sinful. However the pro-gay clergy put their own interpretation to these passages.

The Leviticus version suggests that any one committing homosexual acts should be killed and since people cannot lawfully be killed nowadays the, clergy say that homosexual practices should be allowed. The Romans' version suggests that a man leaving the 'natural use of a woman and transferring to that of a man is a vile affection'. Here the gay-supporting clergy translate this to mean that one is only sinning if the person involved has been married.

These are typical examples showing how clergy can rewrite the Bible to suit their wishes.

It would be interesting to see how they cope with 1 Corinthians 6:9 which says, 'Know ye not that the unright-eous shall not inherit the Kingdom of God: Be not deceived: neither fornicators, nor idolaters, nor adulterers, nor effeminate, nor abusers of themselves with mankind.' Or Leviticus 18:22 which says, 'Thou shall not lie with mankind as with woman kind; it is an abomination.' Or 1 Corinthians 7:2, 'Nevertheless to avoid fornication let every man have his own wife, and let every woman have her own husband.'

(ii) Christ did not die on the Cross

During the 19th century it was suggested that Christ did not die on the cross. He was supposed to have fainted and was in a swoon when placed in the burial chamber. He then came to life in the cold atmosphere of the tomb. Since this idea was first mooted, roughly every decade since doctors have come along suggesting the same theory and presented their arguments as though they were their own thoughts. Again here we have two doctors who suggest an idea which has been in existence for many years.

It is recommended that any one in doubt about the resurrection should read the book *Who moved the Stone* by Frank Morrison. Mr Morrison set out to show that the crucifixion and resurrection of Christ was mainly fiction but after a detailed examination of the Bible record and other sources of information accepted that Jesus did rise from the dead.

Consider the details as recorded in the Bible; it is most unlikely that so many persons (both friends and enemies) should have mistaken Christ being still alive. Experienced soldiers, the centurion sent by Pilate to make sure, the Christians who took down the body from the Cross wrapping it in burial clothes and taking it to the tomb and the Jews who would not have believed Christ was dead if he was not.

Moreover, the tomb was guarded by Roman soldiers who would have made sure the body could not escape by normal means.

Consider the possibility that he was still alive. He is supposed to have recovered consciousness, rolled away the large heavy stone covering the tomb and left the burial chamber without help. (His enemies would not have aided him in any way and his friends would have been aware of any deception.) He would have ripped off his burial clothes which would have been stiff with myrrh and instead of receiving nursing and medical treatment walked 12 miles with pierced feet to Emmaus and back. One should also take into consideration that he had been most cruelly treated before his crucifixion. The same evening he must have appeared to his disciples so completely recovered that instead of looking ill and distressed he had completely recovered. Such a rapid recovery cannot possibly be explained by normal means.

One verification that Christ did die on the Cross arises from research on the Turin Shroud. Originally, by using carbon-dating methods, scientists said the shroud was a medieval delusion. However, the wrong piece of the cloth had been used in the experiment and further tests proved otherwise. By comparing the shroud with a headcloth known to date from the time of Christ, it was suggested that the shroud did date from the first century. It was demonstrated that it had been packed in a cylindrical jar, a method common to the time of Christ's crucifixion. Apparently the stitching used on the shroud was not of the type used in medieval times. Hence it would seem that the Turin Shroud was in fact used on Christ. According to one scientist the amount of blood on the shroud from 100 lacerations, together with that from the hands and feet, would indicate that it was in fact Christ's and would mean that he must have been dead.

In fact, after his crucifixion Jesus was not a normal human being. He was more like a spirit since he could appear and disappear as he wished. He could appear as a human being and take food and then disappear as a spirit being. But surely the most definite proof of his resurrection is the words he spoke to the robber by his side: 'Today shalt thou be with me in paradise.' Since there is no evidence of the thief still living, Jesus must have been referring to heaven. Anyone suggesting there was no resurrection is implying that Jesus was telling lies.

(iii) No belief in the Virgin Birth

Apparently a former Bishop of Durham gave the impression that he did not believe in the virgin Birth. It is difficult to understand why. It may be he thought such a process was impossible. But doctors nowadays can organise all kinds of gestation. Is he saying that God cannot do what man can?

Maybe he thought such a birth was unnecessary. But his miraculous birth from a virgin was essential. He had to have one human parent or he would not have been able to share our human feelings and experience temptation. With two human parents he could not have overcome all the temptations he experienced. He had to have one divine parent to consider himself the Son of God. Even as a 12-year-old boy be referred to his Heavenly Father. Anyone doubting the Virgin Birth is saying that Jesus is committing heresy by referring to God as his Father.

Surely if God came to earth in human form something unusual must have happened.

700 years before the birth of Christ, Isaiah the prophet, said, 'Behold a virgin shall conceive and bear a son.' Does the Bishop question this prophecy?

It was reported that the Bishop only made his comment to make people think. How stupid! The genuine Christian would say what a silly man, the atheist would throw his hat in the air and say, I told you the Bible was a lot of lies, but the person considering becoming a Christian would say, 'if a Bishop does not believe in the Bible, why should I?'

(iv) Living in sin is no longer sinful

The article written by the Rt Rev Alan Morgan, Bishop of Sherwood, and the Rt Rev James Thompson, representing the Church of England Board for Social Responsibilities, indicated that unmarried couples should not only be welcome into the Church but the Church should learn from them. It has never been reported that an unmarried couple have been barred from a Church of England institution but it is more likely that unmarried couples do not wish to go to church. What we are supposed to learn from an unmarried couple is questionable.

Perhaps the two clerics will explain what is meant by 'committed': a short-term agreement living in the same house or an obligation for life? If the latter, there is no reason why they should not marry and set up a stable family relationship. The argument used by the clerics that the couple may be afraid of commitment would suggest that they should not be living together in the first place. Statistics show that couples who have lived together before marriage are more likely to split up after.

The article referred to is helping the alarming trend to single-parent families where any resulting child is likely to become delinquent and the parent overworked. Apparently 40 per cent of children are born outside marriage. Would the reverends like to see this figure increase?

It was reported that Dr Rowan Williams, Archbishop of Canterbury, agreed with some of his bishops that marriage is unnecessary in a constant and faithful relationship. What an acceptance by the leaders of the Church of England to dispense with the sanctity of a ceremony which has been the cornerstone of Christian family life for 1,000 years. It was pointed out that the word 'marriage' does not appear in Genesis. However, the word 'wife' occurs many times and a 'wife' is not possible, without marriage.

It would seem that the clergy involved are leading the way for same sex couples to have the same status, rights and privileges as normal two sex married people. Even two sisters living together would have the same importance

D.H. Lawrence the author of *Lady Chatterley's Lover*, knew the importance of marriage. He said, 'It is marriage which has given man the best of freedom, given him his little Kingdom of his own within the big Kingdom of State, given him his foothold of independence on which to stand and resist an unjust State.'

Jesus himself had no doubt the commitment necessary for two people to live together. He said, 'God made them male and female and for this cause a man shall leave his father and mother, and they shall twain be one flesh. What therefore God has joined together let no man put asunder.'

But Jesus would seem to be outdated nowadays.

(v) Modern Behaviour

The most Rev Richard Holloway, Bishop of Edinburgh, suggests that we should be prepared to alter the standards we have lived with up to now to accommodate the social changes of modern times. He quotes such changes as the appointment of lady doctors and ministers and the introduction of foreign people into jobs considered as the forte of the British and so on. What he does not emphasise is that none of these changes affect our moral standard of living. He then goes on to suggest that our moral standard of living, as set by the Bible, should drop to that of the average shared by the population.

He suggests that if sufficient people are engaged in a particular activity, be it unchristian or not it should be accepted. He agrees with people living, together whether they are the same sex or not even if they are not married. Carrying on with this argument in a few years time we would be expected to accept bigamy, rape, paedophilia etc., providing sufficient people are involved.

Apparently it is now acceptable for children as young as nine or ten years of age to be made aware of sexual intercourse. Various progressive bodies find it necessary to ensure that it is the child's prerogative (apparently necessity) for children to learn about sex as soon as possible and the government and education authorities agree. As expected, the results are numbers of teenage pregnancies, which often result in abortions, and an epidemic of venereal diseases. Maybe the people involved should remember what Jesus said about the influence on children. 'It were better for him that a millstone were hanged about his neck and cast into the sea than he should offend one of these little ones.'

Regrettably, the Church is following fashion rather than resisting the ebb and flow of modern trends. Divorce, Sunday trading and sport have been accepted without a whisper of protest and now the clergy are using these Sunday operations as an excuse for falling attendances at Church services: If the Church goes along with every whim of the population it will become irrelevant.

The biblical scholar and translator of the New Testament Dr William Barclay proclaimed, 'There is no way of making Jesus Christ a supporter of a permissive society, the people will have neither respect or use of a Church that is always trying to conform to it.'

(vi) Doubts on the Resurrection

Previous comments under the heading 'Christ did not die on the Cross' emphasise that the only possible explanation for the action of Christ after his crucifixion was that a supernatural event had occurred.

Consider the effect on his followers after his crucifixion:

When Mary Magdalene saw the vision by the tomb, wishful thinking may have led her to mistake a gardener for Jesus. But apparently she did the opposite, she mistook the resurrected Jesus for the gardener. The two disciples travelling to Emmaus would hopefully have mistaken the stranger for Jesus. But they mistook Jesus for a stranger. These happenings emphasise that these followers were sure that Jesus had died on the Cross.

At the moment Christ died, nothing could have appeared so despondent or hopeless to the people who knew him. They had only a few feeble followers; one had specifically denied him and the more devoted had forsaken him. They were wretched and helpless. They owned not a single synagogue between them. How was it that these plain and innocent few overcame the enmity of the people around them and set out to conquer Kings and their armies and overcame the world? There can only be one explanation: the resurrection of Jesus. How otherwise would his few followers invest the person of Christ with attributes never before designated to anyone?

Jesus appeared at least 12 times after his death, mainly to his disciples, but also Mary Magdalene and the two Marys. According to St Paul, over 500 people saw Jesus after his death. If he had died a normal death, where is his body? His followers would surely want to venerate his grave.

St Paul himself said, 'If Christ be not risen our preaching is in vain.' It is certain that St Paul did not consider his testimony to Jesus to be in vain.

13

The Clergy

Nowadays some clergy are doing their utmost to belittle the Bible. Many do not believe in Creation, they water down the ten commandments to suit their own feelings and their standards conflict with those set by the Bible. One Bishop said he did not believe in the Virgin Birth, an Archbishop cast doubts on the Resurrection and a vicar has even been known to say he did not believe in God. The amazing result of these views is the fact that there did not seem any real concerted objection from the rest of the clergy. If the clergy cannot withhold the standards set by the Bible there is little chance of the normal person doing so.

Professor J.B. Haldane, a notable scientist and one-time marxist said, 'The Bible claims from beginning to end to be the inspired, infallible word of God. Either this claim is true or false. There is no halfway position. If it is false there is no foundation for Christianity. If it is true then Christians are obliged to accept all the Bible.' If only the present day clergy would understand this.

Many of the younger clergy have no respect for Church buildings. They abolish Sunday Schools to lighten their duties and provide services which include children and adults. They rip out seats which have been in existence for hundreds of years and re-arrange to allow spaces for games, dances and other social activities. So that instead of a Church being a centre of reverence and prayer it becomes a social centre and place for a light-hearted view of religion which is non-lasting. These clergy often have no respect for articles which have been dedicated in memory of someone, the argument being that the person is now dead, but they may not necessarily be forgotten by family members who have all devoted their lives to the ongoing of the Church.

I do not remember any concerted effort from the clergy to resist any of the following:

Divorce
Abortion
Cloning (animals and humans)
Marriage outside the Church
Downgrading of teaching Christianity in Schools
Explicit sexual behaviour in the media
Proliferation of gambling casinos
Involvement of young children in sexual knowledge.

However, we do know the Synod has met since the members are suggesting marriage is unnecessary and they have used a tremendous amount of energy to get normal people to agree that homosexuality is also normal.

The amazing thing about the collapse of Christianity is that it is the Christians themselves who have caused the decline. If the clergy was asked if they believed that God took human flesh in the person of Jesus, only a few would give an emphatic yes. The standards set by the Bible are being eroded by clergy who believe in going along with the tide rather than supporting Christian principles. The Pope has said that if faith continues to decline at the present rate, in 70 years' time there will be no Christians left. The majority of the higher echelon of clergy in the Church of England seem to be politically motivated and have little interest in spiritual gospel.

In the BBC Programme 'What the world thinks of Christianity', a survey showed that religion in the United Kingdom is in its demise. Only 46 per cent in this country said they believed in God. The average over ten countries was 73 per cent. Only 21 per cent attend religious services in this country and this figure was the lowest in the poll except for Russia. The highest attendance was 91 per cent in Nigeria, which could mean missionaries from Africa could set us back on a reasonable track.

In 2 Timothy 4:4 Paul wrote, 'They will turn away their ears from the truth and turn aside to myths.' He could be referring to many of our Christian leaders. It is time the Church of England spent its effort preaching the Christian religion instead of trying to accommodate every minor group which happens to come along.

Where are the clergy who will tell us right from wrong, sinners to repentance and give a moral lead?

14

The Media

As a general rule the press, radio and television are not supportive of Christianity. This is probably because the most outspoken writers and broadcasters are scientists and there is probably a lack of forthrightness from the clergy.

Following are a few examples of items which have appeared in the daily press and do not seem to been answered by the Christian fraternity.

One article 'The dying Mythology of Christ' suggested that Christianity was not an established religion and Christ was a mythological figure.

Another article explained that the Theory of Everything – a formula following on from Darwin's Theory of Evolution and Einstein's Theory of Relativity will explain the answers to all life's mysteries and finally dispel the idea of God.

Again, an article called 'The fitting survival of Darwin's Theory' drove mankind off his God-given pedestal and put us among the beasts and birds where we belong.

These kind of features are read and believed by many people and there does not appear as often similar articles supporting Christianity. Often articles appear supporting evolution, particularly when part of a human skeleton is dug up. Such a discovery is front-page news but when the item discovered is found to be false the error is ignored or relegated to a small almost insignificant paragraph.

Regarding radio, there is usually a short religious programme each morning but the main programme for the discussion of Christian values is the 'Thought for Today' which is allowed two minutes of a three-hour programme. The speakers do not always have pronounced views and sometimes seem to have a fear to express their ideas in case they annoy someone. Even this almost insignificant programme is attacked by people such as Richard Dawkins, the evolutionist, Ludovic Kennedy, the broadcaster, and Polly Toynbee, the journalist, who say that views of atheists should be allowed to be included. It would be much more sensible for these cynics to have their own programme and leave the spot allocated to Christianity to be fixed.

Television is the most regarded of the three media and hence has the most influence on people's lives. Unfortunately, the programmes have descended into the involvement of explicit sex, swearing and general immoral behaviour. Christians may not like such degradation, but they just have to tolerate what is apparently necessary to boost 'Viewers' numbers'. Occasionally, BBC and ITV do produce an enlightening programme but somehow they do not leave the Christian entirely happy.

In one programme scientists demonstrated that Sodom and Gomorrah had existed and the remains proved that a catastrophe had occurred. The sort of evidence that emphasised the Bible account. But just as the programme was being switched off a female voice said words to the effect the whole episode could have been just a legend, contradicting what had been proved.

In one TV programme 'The Testing of God', there were several notable scientists explaining that we could do without God. The support on behalf of God consisted of one priest who was only allowed to comment for two thirds of the programme and a lady cleric who admitted she wasn't sure about God anyway. The programme could have been compared with the trial of a prisoner supported by two weak witnesses but opposed by several famous lawyers, The witness, of course, not being allowed to speak on his own behalf.

One BBC programme in their Horizon series, called the 'Bible Code' was so distorted against the Bible that it left one wondering why it was broadcast. Details of the Bible Code are explained in the chapter 'Bible Puzzles' but the account in the BBC programme was so biased that it was clear an attempt was made to rubbish the findings. The prediction of Yitzhak Rabin's death and the details of Princess Diana's accident were not shown. What the programme did emphasise is that any message can be derived by picking out the letters at random from a book, but did not stress that in the Bible Code the letters are chosen mathematically and predict future happenings which the random method does not. The programme omitted to stress that important people such as the Chief of Mossad, Yasser Aarafat, top intelligence officials of the US National Security Agency all take the code seriously, in fact it appeared that the BBC did not believe in the Bible Code and deliberately omitted all the positive arguments giving support to the Bible Code. This on their flagship series 'Horizon'. Can we ever be sure of a programme with an unbiased report?

On Sunday evening 21st March 2004 the BBC put on a televised programme called 'The Flood' which was a criticism of the Bible story of Noah's Ark. It demonstrated quite clearly how the BBC is biased against Christianity.

The programme said the Ark could not have been built entirely of wood since wood was not strong enough, it could not have floated on water, all the animals on earth could not have been accommodated. Even if the ice caps melted there would not have been enough water to cover the hills. It also alleged that no real evidence had ever been found of the existence of the Ark. All leading to a condemnation of the Bible story.

What is the truth?

Comparing weight for weight the strength of wood is roughly as strong as metal. In other words, providing the appropriate cross section of wood is chosen it could be equally as strong as steel and the Ark would be strong enough for its purpose. It must be realised that Noah spent 100 years building the Ark so that it would be well built. Any hull of a ship made from wood or steel would float and there is no reason to suppose that in this case it would fail. In addition to the base area, it had two decks which not only increased the strength of the Ark but gave it a total support area of 11,000 square yards. This area was split into compartments to accommodate the animals. According to some reports there were about one million species to be placed, but two thirds of these were insects and two per cent were fish and reptiles which could have existed outside the Ark. Birds and the smaller animals would not take up much room and the larger animals could have been represented by subspecies. (One pair of cats could account for all the cats, one pair of apes could have been the ancestors of chimpanzees, gorillas etc.) With regard to shortage of water the Bible says, 'All the fountains of the deep were broken up and the windows of heaven were open.' There was also rain for 40 nights and days. It is recorded in the second day of creation that 'water was gathered under heaven into one place'. It follows there would be a tremendous amount of water and the hills could easily be covered since they may not have been so high in Noah's time. Earth scientists are continually pointing out how land masses have changed and how hills have been formed by erupting land. Atheist scientists are always saying that there is no evidence of a large earth flood. However, shells taken from the bottom of the Black Sea prove that there had indeed, been a sudden change from fresh water to salt water some 7,500 years ago.

The transitional layer between fresh and salt water sediments was less than one millimetre thick, proving that the switch must have been instantaneous. In 1993 William Ryan and Walter Pitman, marine biologists from Columbia University in America, found, close to the coastline of the Black Sea, evidence of sun-bleached shells, plant roots and a layer of mud. This is powerful evidence that the land surface had been flooded. They also suggested that since the flood waters must have risen so rapidly, the old lake shoreline should still exist but deep below the waters of the sea. In 1999 ocean explorer Robert Ballard used sonar and remote controlled underwater cameras to find an ancient shoreline 167 metres deep exactly where Ryan and Pitman had predicted. This was proof that the flood was real. Of course the BBC programme did not mention these findings. With regard to lack of evidence of the remains of the Ark, there are plenty of possible sightings. In 1949 an American spy plane showed a grainy image at the summit of Mount Ararat in eastern Turkey. At 15,000 ft above sea level the image showed what appeared to be a man-made structure some 400 ft long. What the shape most resembled was that of a ship. One summer, a heatwave hung over the north-east of Europe which melted tons of ice from the top of Mount Ararat, thus exposing objects never seen before. Daniel McGivern, a Christian businessman claimed that a man-made object appeared and he intends to investigate further. It follows that the remains of the Ark may be found eventually.

However, another red herring was introduced:

The presenters tried to show that Bible story was a myth and simply an ancient legend by describing the story of the Epic of Gilgamesh of ancient Mesopotania. Apparently a farmer built a large boat to carry beer, animals and grain along the river Euphrates and during a storm it foundered on Bahrain. If this boat was as large as the Ark it would take a tremendous number of rowers to row it upstream and certainly it is a less likely story than Noah's Ark. What these anti-Christian people cannot appreciate is that God who made the world can easily manage an Ark and a Flood.

One enlightening religious programme is the BBC's 'Songs of Praise' which is a 35 minutes episode on Sunday evening. It used to be a source of comfort for old people who could not attend Church but took pleasure in the singing of hymns they knew so well. However, it is developing into more of a variety show and to show how television presenters regard the importance of this programme the timing is altered almost every week, thus causing much confusion.

How pleasant it would be for Christians to have a regular religious programme with a genuine Christian person supporting the Christian religion.

15

Free Will

Several times in this book the term 'free will' has been used to emphasise that we are able to decide our own destiny. Generally most decisions we have to make are not morally important: do we mow the lawn today or tomorrow? Do we paint the house white or blue? However, free will does become important when a moral decision has to be made. Is what we choose to do wrong or acceptable?

The cynics say that although Christians are supposed to have 'free will' they are always expected to do God's will and therefore, are not free to act at all. But the choice to please God or ignore him is always present. If we choose to enter a den of iniquity, God will not physically prevent us from entering. As Christians we always want to please God and do his will but we are not forced to do so.

God could have made man such that he could do no wrong, but in this case we would have been robots and not able to make our own decisions. But we are not robots and wouldn't want to be. So that we are able to decide individually what we want to do or say and are often left with a choice to do good or evil.

However, real freedom is not doing what we like. We should think of the responsibility of what we are doing and be aware of how our actions may affect other people. Freedom without discipline results in confusion and disorder. A free country is not one without laws or punishment for wrong doings, but one which is governed democratically for the good of all people.

Decisions are sometimes difficult to make. Do we play golf or visit a friend ill in hospital? A game of golf may be necessary to offer relaxation after a hard time but the ill friend should never be forgotten. Never should a friend be persuaded to act against his will if his choice is an ethical one. We should never dissuade someone from carrying out good deeds.

Free will is a precious endowment and should always be used with honour and justice.

16

Creation versus Evolution

There are two main ways in which it is assumed that the earth and its life forms were formed. The creationist assumes that God created everything as explained in Genesis.

The evolutionist supports Darwin and says that God had no influence in the development, but a spark of life appeared somehow on the Earth and all types of life developed from that spark. There are a few people who assume some life forms developed naturally but God did have some influence. We must assume, however, that God would have total influence or not at all.

Hundreds of books and thousands of articles have been written on the creation–evolution issue, some supporting one development and some the other.

Generally Christians support the creation theory whilst evolutionists are usually atheistic scientists who cannot tolerate the thought of God being involved in any way. Of course, the scientists would prefer the evolution route because it gives them scope for research.

Since no humans were alive when life began on Earth neither of the two theories can be proved conclusively so we can only decide by the evidence available. I have no intention of getting involved with scientific arguments since science without positive proof is of no consideration.

Human beings are the ultimate in the development of

animals and it is interesting to note the difference in definition of man by the atheist and the Christian.

The British archaeologist and scientist Dr S.B. Leakey, defined man as follows: 'To qualify as a man there must be reasonably good evidence to suggest that the creature made tools to a set and regular pattern'. Note the term 'reasonably good evidence' indicates what the scientist thinks and not what he knows – simply a man is an animal that uses tools.

Now Christians define a man by referring to the Bible. 'So God created man in his own image in the image of God created he him.'

In particular the three attributes that separate the scientist 'man' and the Christian one are:

(1) Ability of abstract thought including art, music, etc.
(2) Morality, love and sense of religion.
(3) Communication with language.

It follows there is a considerable void between the evolutionist man and the creation one.

The problem with scientists is that they put forward ideas without any positive proof and often their theories are found to be wrong.

In addition to saying incorrectly that substances such as DDT, thalidomide do humans no harm, they make wild statements about evolution. They find a skeleton and say, 'We have pushed our known origins back to more than three million years ago.' A skeleton of a boy of four becomes 'the true origin of the modern human race.' A jawbone 2.33 million years old is hailed as the earlier evidence of the human family. Such statements are common and often found to be nonsense . At one time Neanderthal men were said to be one of our ancestors. Apparently they died out 30,000 years ago.

In August 2003, when the sea exposed the intricate patterns etched on a slab of granite in the sea at Gorleston near Great Yarmouth, Norfolk, the experts could, hardly contain their excitement. The archaeologists took photographs, consulted their colleagues and estimated the carvings had been made around 2,000 years ago. Translated, the runes revealed the message, 'This stone is for people who celebrate with fire.' Then a gentleman by the name of Barry Luxton admitted to carving the etchings. He had completed them eight years previously.

Then we come to our development from apes. For over 200 years we have been told by the scientists that we have evolved from apes. In fact, in the science laboratory of almost every senior school in Britain there has been a picture illustrating this fact, an ape-like figure body bent and front arms touching the ground is shown in various attitudes straightening up and becoming less and less hairy until the final figure is that of a man. Unfortunately for the evolutionist, this indication is now known to be complete nonsense. In 1971 Dr Peter Pearson of the Population Genetics Unit at Oxford University suggested that man, gorilla, and chimpanzee all had a common ancestor. Many scientists ignored his theories because it didn't follow the evolution plan. However modern DNA studies here proved that Dr Pearson was correct and chimpanzee, gorillas, orang-utan and man all share the same ancestor and developed at the same time.

It follows that we should not accept the views of scientists unless they have absolute proof of their theories.

I ask a few questions which would seem to upset the evolution idea but to which I have never found an adequate answer:

(1) Where did water come from? All scientists will accept that water is necessary for the development of life and yet there would not seem to have had a natural development. In his book *A Brief History of Time* Stephen Hawkin states that

originally the earth was at a high temperature without atmosphere and emitting hydrogen gas and hydrogen sulphide. There would seem to be no possibility of water developing under these circumstances and yet later on he refers to seas with no indication how they developed. Moses knew how important water was and indicates its presence in the second verse of the Bible.

(2) Why have we got two eyes? Carl Sagan, the American evolutionist in his book *Cosmos*, explains how the eye could have developed. Richard Dawkins, the English counterpart, in his book *The Blind Watchmaker* has a much more complex explanation. However, neither explains why nearly all living beings have two eyes. By natural selection only one eye would have expected and this might have sufficed. I knew a gentleman who had lost the sight of one eye and who lived a normal life. We could ask the same question about, ears, lungs and kidneys. In the latter case we can afford to give one kidney away and still live a normal life. In every case – eyes, ears, lungs and kidneys – there are advantages in having two. Two eyes enable distances to be estimated more accurately, one lung may cease to function satisfactorily but the other one may suffice to keep the person alive, God in his wisdom may have seen the possibility of someone giving one kidney away to save the life of someone else. In these dual arrangements it would seem that design was involved, in which case, evolution does not fit into the scheme of things.

There are examples where the development by evolution is difficult to appreciate.

The defence method of a bombardier beetle requires hydrogen and hydroquinone to be mixed to form a spray to blast its predators. How were these substances developed and gradually mixed in the correct proportions by a development process?

The woodpecker hammers at the trunk of a tree ten times per second for six hours. Any other creature would have its

86

skull shattered. The woodpecker has a 'shock absorber' between its beak and its cranium. As the beak hits the tree a muscle pulls the cranium back. But to reach the insects inside the tree it has a tongue five times as long as a normal bird. It has to have a unique design to store the tongue without choking itself. The hyoid bone that controls the tongue passes through the lower jaw up behind and over the cranium and is anchored in the front nostril. The tongue is coated with a sticky substance and is similar to a spearhead with a number of backward pointing barbs. How could such a complicated arrangement become operational by normal means?

A mother whale has an extraordinary nipple which is necessary to feed its babies under water without them taking in sea water. The nipple is designed to allow such an operation. How could it have developed naturally?

These examples create problems for the evolutionists since the developments do not appear possible by gradual evolution. The answer by the evolutionary scientists is that anything can happen within three million years. However, examples chosen seem to suggest that design is involved and if this is so, evolution is untenable.

Many scientists are beginning to change their mind regarding evolution.

W.R. Thompson, a known evolutionist said, 'The success of Darwinism was accomplished by a decline in scientific integrity.'

Many evolutionists such as the late Stephen Gould have ditched Darwin and considered 'punctuated equilibrium', which is roughly equivalent to a reptile's egg hatching out as a bird.

It is interesting to note that as scientific knowledge develops, scientists still have differing opinions. Regarding the DNA code, Richard Dawkins, the eminent evolutionist, was heard to say that the code allows us to do without God. This statement is without knowledge of the means as to how the code developed. However, Francis Crick, who together with James Watson, discovered the structure of the DNA code admitted that the discovery proved it must have been the work of a creating God.

17

Other Religions

There are many religions throughout the world and even quite a number in this country. There are Hinduism, Baha'i, Jainism etc. which do not have much support. The main religions in this country to be considered are Christianity, Judaism, and Islam. Christianity is divided into two sects, Roman Catholic and Protestant, but only Christianity is considered necessary at this stage.

The Trinity doctrine is unique to the Christian Religion. Some religions did have a group of three gods but it was a form of polytheism and not to be compared with the Christian 'Father, Son and Holy Ghost'.

Incarnation is said to resemble doctrines in other religions but, as stated in the book *Living Religions* by A.R. Stedman, 'Christianity is founded, not as Judaism on a law to be observed, nor as Islam on a book to be memorised nor as Confucianism on a code to be followed nor as Buddhism on a collection of teachings, but a life to be lived.' It follows that the Holy Bible expresses what Christians endeavour to emulate is to attempt to imitate Christ.

The Bible is the source of inspiration, and guidance for good living of Christians. The Old Testament was developed over a period of years from approximately 1000 BC to roughly 400 BC, giving the history of the kings of the whole nation, the kings of Judah and the kings of Israel. This history was recorded by about 17 prophets, with Moses the first one, recording events back to 4000 BC. As explained elsewhere, the writings of these prophets must have been influenced by God. The New Testament was written mainly by five apostles from 42 AD to 100 AD.

The development of Judaism is in the Old Testament of the Bible. The creed of Judaism is based on the concept of a transcendent and omnipotent one true God. They believe his will to be indicated in the Torah, which is a written script and is the Hebrew name for the law of Moses. This law was divinely revealed to Moses on Mount Sinai. Jews also consider the Talmud, which includes the civil and canonical laws which is a collection of oral comments and criticisms by Jewish Rabbis. They reject the idea of incarnation.

The sacred book of Islam is the Koran, said to be written on the orders of God by Mohammed, who was a married man. He accepted the inspiration of the Old Testament and claimed to be a successor to Moses. Moslems are aware of their duties. They perform prescribed acts of worship and strive to fulfil good works. They have five obligatory prayer sequences each day as well as other non-obligatory ones. They fast during Ramadam and pilgrimage to Mecca.

All Moslems have a religious obligation to marry and form a family, whereas in Christianity the apostle said it's better to remain single and only get married if considered necessary.

Only Christians accept Jesus Christ to be the son of God since in Judaism and Islam he is only considered as a prophet.

The big question remains: can the various religions be combined in some way? There seems to be some effort by the Church of England clergy to attempt such an operation.

Ostensibly, Jews, Christians and Moslems worship the same God and hence it might be expected for all members to live peaceably together. Unfortunately, this is not so. Even

Protestant and Catholic Christians have sometimes found it necessary to oppose each other and occasionally the animosity has led to war. Christians and Jews have not always found it possible to live together in harmony. Unfortunately, the more radical Moslems are hostile to other religions and seem determined to eliminate them. It must be said that the majority of all the members of all religions are prepared to live peacefully together. This situation did exist about 1,400 years ago. Near Mount Sinai is a Christian monastery founded by the emperor Justinian. This monastery was in Muslim territory and for centuries it has been guarded by the local Bedouin. Muslim caliphs had supported the Christian monks and even supported the Jewish academy in Jerusalem, indicating that it is possible for people of different faiths to live together.

It is possible for members of different religions to be happy in each other's company, but it is much more difficult to expect each religion to be modified to create a common base.

The Bishop of Oxford said, 'Leaders of other faiths need to be much more than guests, they need to be present at the sanctuary at the centre of things.' This is rather an ambitious target and one which is unlikely to be fulfilled since all religions have there own codes of conduct and sacred services which are unique to each. To modify the procedures so that two religions could be interlinked would considerably weaken both.

The Christian religion expects its members to be baptised into membership and continued in membership by being confirmed. Confirmation allows communion in the form of bread and wine into the body and blood of Christ in memory of the Crucifixion as a full, perfect and sacrifice oblation and satisfaction for the sins of the whole world. The two sacraments of baptism and communion represent the action of God towards man, not man towards God. In other words, baptism is God's acceptance of man into his Church, and communion is Christ giving himself to his believers.

Since other religions do not accept Jesus as the Son of God, it is difficult to see how their members can be welcomed into the Church as Christians.

Referring to the Church of England communion service Jesus said, 'Do this in remembrance of me,' which is a command and not an optional extra.'

18

Back to the Bible

To get back to realise the importance of the Bible we must believe that it is the Word of God from beginning to end. All positive evidence would seem to show that it is a true history and God must have influenced its writings. How else could the prophets have foretold what would happen thousands of years after their death? How could Christianity have grown to influence so much of the world if the Bible was false? How can anyone say that the events in the Bible never took place when archaelogists continue to verify that the stories are accurate? How can anyone say that Jesus Christ was not a good man? If so much of the Bible is shown to be true with no positive contradictions then it must be assumed to be true throughout its writings.

Unfortunately there are many people and even some clergy who find fault with parts of the Bible although they have no definite reason to question its authority.

Clergy should not publicly question any part of the Bible unless they have emphatic proof that there is something amiss, since such views only cause confusion. For a bishop to doubt the Virgin Birth or an archbishop to query the Resurrection is tantamount to saying the Bible is false and thus misleading the lay person. Some clergy question the possibility of creation as the start and development of life but they should not state their views in public. After all, many eminent scientists accept the creation story.

APPENDIX

The da Vinci Code

During the 1980s Michael Baigent together with co-authors Richard Leigh and Henry Lincoln wrote a book titled *The Holy Blood and The Holy Grail*. Essentially it was an attempt to show that Christ survived his crucifixion and lived to get married and fathered children. Mary Magdalene was supposed to have been his wife, but Mary of Bethany and her sister were also suggested possible spouses. According to the book, during his time on the cross Christ was not offered a sponge saturated with vinegar as indicated in the Bible, but one containing a drug which put him to sleep and enabled him to be removed from the cross while still alive. This would have involved a conspiracy by all the people concerned with the crucifixion; Pontius Pilate, Joseph of Arimathea, the Roman soldiers, the Jews etc. The Jews certainly would not have allowed such an action.

Anyone tending to believe this account should read the chapters in this book headed 'Jesus did not die on the Cross' and 'Doubts on the Resurrection'. In the context of this book the 'Holy Grail' refers to the bloodline of Christ and not the cup used at the last supper.

Don Brown took the basic idea of the above myth and wrote his version in the form of a novel. Unfortunately many people believed it to be the truth and antichristian experts hailed it as a serious stumbling block to the Bible story.

What is the truth:

Many people have been involved with research into the details in the book and invariably considered them as very doubtful and not substantiated. The BBC asked Tony Robinson to look into the matter and he found all the important features involved to be fictitious.

The artist Leonardo da Vinci was introduced into the story as being involved with the codes and messages relating to the 'Holy Grail' so that his pictures have been investigated to note if any evidence of secret knowledge is evident. The picture which would involve the 'Holy Grail' is the *Last Supper*. This picture shows Christ with his disciples at the supper table before he was crucified. The antichristians point out that the person to the right of Christ has feminine features and hence, according to the unbelievers, to be Mary Magdalene.

Now consider what would seem to be the truth. The picture involved is not a photograph but a picture painted 1400 years after the event. Clearly, da Vinci used artistic licence. Instead of showing the disciples sitting round the table, as one would expect, they are all situated down one side. No doubt he painted one of the disciples looking gentle and tender as a contrast to some of the heavy-featured others. The disciple under discussion does not appear to have feminine hands.

There were 12 disciples at the supper and da Vinci shows 12 people in addition to Christ. If one of them was substituted by Mary Magdalene then one disciple was missing and this is not possible. The cynic would say that Judas had left but this is not likely since his absence would have indicated his betrayal of Christ.

The whole story is based on a priest becoming rich because of his knowledge of the Christ bloodline. Tony Robinson said there was some evidence that he gained his money by selling places in heaven to gullible people.